How to Make a Fortune Working from Home

How to Make a Fortune Working from Home

Deborah Bowers

ISBN: 978-0-9926493

ISBN: 978-0-9926493-1-9

Published by self-published author Deborah Bowers.
Revised edition 2015

Dedication

With special thanks to my

family

I dedicate this book to family life and to those who need to work from home.

CONTENTS

1. It Costs Nothing   11

2. Write a Book   14

3. Selling on Amazon   24

4. Domain Names   29

5. Free Websites   33

6. Web Hosting   35

7. Affiliate Marketing   38

8. Drop Shipping   41

9. Setting up a Company   48

10. Sourcing Products   51

11. Getting into Stores   54

12. Marketing   60

13. Helpful Tips   63

14. What Next?   68

Acknowledgements

I thank my family and friends for their patience and encouragement as I devoted my time and effort to writing this book. I hope that it will help many who must remain at home for personal reasons, to raise a family or for any other reason, to earn an income, whilst utilising the benefits of technology and the information age.

I also thank the founder of the worldwide web, Sir Tim Berners-Lee, who has made it possible for information to be available and accessible to all at the touch of a button or the click of a mouse.

The world of work is changing. The demands of work and family life can create challenges that leave us wondering which one to choose. The aim of this book is to make those two challenges compatible and help you excel in both areas without spending a fortune.

Introduction

If you are reading this book, you must be interested in earning a living working from home.

I know that this book can set you on the right path and save you money. Here you will learn to earn a living by utilising the Internet. This sort of information is, usually controlled by corporations who charge you thousands to enrol on their training program. More often than not you are in desperate need of the money they are charging you and they encourage you to use your credit card, thereby plunging you into further debt. What they are really doing is preying on your vulnerability and your need for financial freedom and security.

To help you pay your debts and start living the debt free life, they plunge you into debt. In the end the only person to profit is the corporation, from the fees you have paid for their assistance.

No longer do you need to get into debt in order to learn how to make a fortune working from home. All you need is the ability to read and use of a computer with Internet access. If you are reading this book right now, you are well on your way to learning how to earn a living working from home.

I guarantee that making a fortune needs not cost you a fortune. After reading this book and following its suggestions, you will see that the advice contained herein works and does not cost you a fortune. You will see your way clearly to accomplish your goals from the comfort of your home.

This book does not promise you overnight success. Neither does it promise that you will achieve success just by reading it and sitting on your couch at home doing nothing. As in all things, following the advice of this book requires perseverance, hard work, patience, and time.

The most rewarding part of the effort is that you will not have to put up with having just any job to pay the bills or a job that makes you fat because it keeps you from managing your work-life balance or a job that takes you away from your kids. Instead, you will be able to work from the comfort of your home and shape the life you have dreamt of whilst earning a living or even making a fortune. You can start earning overnight, without spending a penny.

The information published here was correct and accurate at the time of writing. The author does not represent the position of any of the websites referred to in this work and will not be bound or liable should circumstances change by the time you read this book.

My hope is that you will learn how to earn a living using the Internet without paying a fortune for it. I cannot teach you all the options available, as there are too many, and you may find other helpful tips not mentioned here. A good reference point, should you need help, is to search for tips and advice to help you accomplish your vision on any of the search engines, available on the Internet. Google is an excellent search engine. Another useful idea is to visit www.youtube.com, where you can always ask the question 'How do I get visitors to my website?' and the like. You are sure to find a free video that gives you plenty of *free* tips.

This book will help you put in place the building blocks to your new life at little or no great financial cost to you. Take some time to read through and start living your dream today.

CHAPTER 1

It Cost Nothing

The cold-callers who contact you, offering to teach you how to 'get rich quick' using the Internet know very well, that it costs only your Internet connection to use the Internet. What you use the Internet for may sometimes cost you a subscription fee or if purchasing products it may cost you the price of the product. With the advent of net neutrality, by Tim Wu, if upheld, searching the Internet should cost no more than your connection fee and/or monthly subscription. Why, then, do cold-callers require you to pay thousands of pounds/dollars to them, to teach you how to search the Internet to start a business or earn a living? I am always surprised at how much they expect you to pay and how keen they are to get you into debt to teach you the tricks of the trade. They assure you that the only equipment you need is a computer and Internet access, but they fail to mention the thousands you need to line their pockets as they teach you to use the World Wide Web.

When I first began to explore the Internet, to find work-from-home options, I was surprised at just how much information is available. All you want to know to start your own work-from-home operation and all you need to know to make yourself a fortune is right at your fingertips on the Internet. All you need is a little patience, dedication and time. I therefore set out to compile this book, as I wanted to benefit all those who wanted more time at home with their kids and for whom the work/life balance had become impossible. Too many people are working just to pay the bills and not because it adds value or satisfaction to their lives.

This book is designed to help you pay your bills and give you back control of your life, which is too often lost to the world of work. You will experience the joy of more family time and the satisfaction of being your own boss.

This work cannot cover every aspect of working from home, nor is that my intention. The areas covered here are those that can be achieved using established businesses, such as eBay, Amazon, Facebook, Twitter, Pinterest and others to market your business.

These established markets are preferred, as all businesses need marketing. You can rest assured that customers visit these sites every day and that they have an international presence. By using these established platforms *you* will have an international presence. These companies are international and are trusted globally, so you will also be building upon their reputation.

To help you achieve your goal, you may need to join a few other international sites, such as PayPal, Alibaba, moneybookers.com, and Lunar pages, to name but a few. You may add your own names based on your experience, but I have suggested these, as they can help you understand what must be in place in order to start this journey to earning a living from home.

CHAPTER 2

Write a Book

The common wisdom is that books do not sell and will not make you rich. If J.K. Rowling had believed this, she would not be a multimillionaire today. The truth is that you do not know what is likely to sell.

The key is to put your best effort into what you do, and leave the rest for the reader to judge. If people like your work, then the sky is the limit.

Take a moment to read the article, 'Self-publishing writer becomes million seller', at http://www.telegraph.co.uk/culture/books/booknews/8589963/ Self-publishing-writer-becomes-million-seller.html#. This story is about the amazing success of John Locke, who is the first self-published author to have sold a million e-books. He didn't stop there; he also wrote an e-book titled *How I sold 1 million e-books in 5 months* for those who want to replicate his success. Everyone wants to know how he did it.

Once you have written your book, get it edited and proofread. Search the Internet for editors and proofreaders. There you can find a range of services and be able to compare prices within your budget.

Once your book has been edited and proofread, and you are comfortable with its standard, the next step is to get it published. There are many options available, but the most frequently visited sites are Amazon and Lulu. Both provide excellent platforms that you can use to publish your material at no cost to you. The sites take a portion of the selling price when your book sells and pay you royalties.

If you are publishing on Lulu.com, all you need to do is visit www.lulu.com. However, Amazon has created separate platforms for making books available on their site. The first option may be to get your book on Kindle, as the use of e-readers is gaining popularity and is the way forward. To do this, visit https://kdp.amazon.com/self-publishing/help, which will tell you how to publish your book on Kindle. The other option is to publish your book at www.createspace.com. This will enable you to make paperback copies of your book available on Amazon. Both methods of publishing are discussed in further detail throughout this chapter.

If you decide to publish your book on Amazon or lulu.com you will be offered the option of a free book cover, and you can chose the cover that suits you. You can also upload your own cover design. Alternatively, both companies offer help with proofreading, editing, book cover design and marketing at a cost. You can also search the Internet via Google for 'free book covers', where you are sure to find options. The advantage of using Amazon and Lulu to assist you is, you are engaging their experts, who will provide you with a cover of international standard that will give the most professional finish to your work. Should you decide to use the covers provided free of charge on these sites, please note that they are limited, but print well when the book is printed in paperback.

All you need to do is follow the formatting instructions and upload your book onto the site. Voila! Your book will be live within twenty-four hours (once the site has approved its content) it will be available for you to proofread. Once you have proofread and accepted the finished product, your book will be available for sale to the whole world, and you would have achieved this without the stress of finding a publisher. Let the public decide whether you become a bestseller. The public will determine your success by the click of a mouse when they download your book or order a hard copy. You can also order copies of your book to retail from Amazon or Lulu.com.

With e-readers becoming ever more popular and set to replace books, a market has been created for the sale of e-books. Next time you travel, take a look at how many people are reading on e-readers like Kindle. At https://kdp.amazon.com/self-publishing you will find a video that takes you through just how easy it is to get your book published on Kindle.

You may write a book on any topic that is of interest to you and get it published. You can keep track of your sales and earn royalties on the world's greatest online platform, Amazon.com. I am certain that you never thought it was that simple or straight forward.

Both amazon.com and lulu.com have free content about how to promote your material. They help you promote your book by giving you free marketing tips and advice. Behind the scenes they also provide a paid service that helps you to create a book trailer promotion, leaflets, and press releases.

There is also plenty of other free content on the Internet that may help you maximize your sales and publicity. One of these is Smashwords. The free *Smashwords Style Guide,* by Mark Coker, gives you tips on how to publish on Smashwords and insights into publishing your e-book. You can also join Smashwords by going to www.smashwords.com/signup. Mark Coker has also published *Smashwords Book Marketing Guide*, which has received a five-star rating.

All of these websites will provide you with a barcode or ISBN number. Your book needs this number to make it marketable anywhere in the world. You can also order your own ISBN from http://www.isbn.nielsenbook.co.uk. Having your own ISBN, allows you to take control and expand your sales by printing copies of your book, with its unique ISBN, for sale should you wish to do so.

There are many other ways to market your e-book. A simple search on the web for how to market or sell an e-book will find many free articles, which will assist you in promoting your book online.

Twitter, Facebook, Pinterest, StumbleUpon, and Reddit are also free marketing tools that can assist you in getting your book into the hands of those who are interested in it. When it comes to the power of social media, a must-read is Claude Bouchard's 'How I Really Got a 1/4 Million Followers'. This article can be found at http://www.claudebouchardbooks.com/apps/blog/show/135347 68-how-i-really-got-a-1-4-million-followers. The article examines how Twitter can be used to reach a wide audience.

Another interesting publication if you are considering publishing a book is an article by David Carnoy of C/NET in which he discusses the ins and outs of self-publishing: 'Self-publishing a book: 25 things you need to know'. This article can be found at http://reviews.cnet.com/self-publishing. Other free options include www.monkeybars.net and www.Pubit.

www.apple.com is also new in the field. You may also wish to load your book onto www.uploadnsell.com, which is a free service. What I love about them is their free newsletter, which keeps you updated about what is selling.

If you would like to write a book but feel that you are not a very good writer, you may wish to engage the services of a ghost-writer, although, these services are not free. With ghost-writing, you work with a writer who will take your content and ideas and put them in book form. Ghost-writing services can be obtained by searching the Internet for ghost-writers or by visiting http://theghostinthemachine.com.

Of course, the focus of this book is to show you just how much you can achieve at no cost. You should pay for a service only if you are sure that the service is something you cannot do yourself or is so time-consuming, that it would not be worth your time. As you have seen throughout this chapter, most, if not all, of what you need, is at your disposal absolutely *free*!

If you are thinking of publishing, here are other useful websites.

www.bookmarket.com/eproducts.htm

This site provides details of many free platforms for publishing your work on the Internet. Remember: the future is digital.

www.publish-yourself.com

This site is mainly for those who are publishing to a UK market. It contains fantastic tips on how to market your product yourself. The writer has had success as a self-publisher, and I am grateful to him for sharing his knowledge and experience.

There are a few companies who can also assist you with publishing you work. A few are named below. They all charge fees. My personal recommendation is that you work with createspace.com and use their experts if you have to, but should you need to look outside www.createspace.com, you may wish to consider the following:

www.authorhouse.com
www.talfordpublishing.com
www.vintagepress.com
www.bookguild.co.uk

www.xulonpress.com.

Should you need help the above mentioned self-publishing companies will work with you to achieve your goal whilst allowing you to keep ownership of your work. They do charge a fee, but you can shop around to ensure that you receive a price within your budget.

If you would like to find a traditional publisher for your book, you will probably first need to find an agent. The websites listed below, can help you find agents who are interested in the subject about which you have written. An important note: You should never pay an agent up front. All legitimate agents take a percentage once they have sold your book to a publisher.
So please be aware when looking for one. There are many other options available. The path you take depends on your personal circumstances. This book seeks only to open your eyes to some available options for consideration. If you are interested in this option you may look up these websites.
www.literarymarketplace.com
www.wlwritersagency.com

CHAPTER 3

Selling on Amazon and eBay

Why sell on Amazon or eBay? It would be wrong to say that selling on Amazon or eBay is free because it is not. You can either pay a commission once your product sells or pay a monthly fee, depending on the platform, to sell as an upgraded seller or pro merchant. The choice as to how you sell is up to you, but the advantage of using such a platform is that you do not have to seek customers; customers visit these platforms seeking your products. This means that you are selling in a global market place; all you need to do is list your product.

Selling on Amazon is easy. Simply visit www.amazon.com or www.amazon.co.uk (if you are located in the United Kingdom). Scroll down to the bottom of the page where you will find the words 'Make Money with Us'. Beneath that heading are the words 'Sell on Amazon'. Click 'Sell on Amazon' and choose between 'Sell a little (basic)' and 'Sell a lot (Pro)'. Then simply follow the instructions and let Amazon teach you how to sell with them. The training is *free*.

Amazon also offers an 'aStore', where you can create your own store containing Amazon products. You can link this store to your website if you have one, so people who are searching your website can link directly to your Amazon store.

The best thing about this option is that you can sell Amazon products or any specialized item without keeping any stock or inventory. Click on the Amazon aStore link to learn more about this option. Once you have registered with Amazon, all you have to do is name your page and select the category of products you wish to sell. Your store goes live, and you are ready to welcome customers.

Amazon also provides webinars to assist those who wish to sell on Amazon. What more can you ask for?

You can also sell products on eBay by visiting www.ebay.com or www.ebay.co.uk. You will first need to register with eBay. Once you have done this, scroll down to the bottom of the page, where you will see the word 'sell'. You will have the option to sell basics, eBay for top-rated sellers, eBay for business, and so on. Take some time to learn how to sell in the category that is of interest to you. Remember: all this training is *free*.

When you sell on eBay, you will be advised to set up a PayPal account to be used in conjunction with your seller's account. PayPal is a safe and easy way to pay for and receive money for goods online. Click on the PayPal link on the eBay site and follow the instructions. You can also go directly to PayPal by visiting www.paypal.com and following the instructions.

When using www.paypal.com, ensure that your county or region is shown in the top right hand corner of the screen. For example, if you are accessing the site from the United Kingdom, you should see on the top right hand corner the British flag, and the words 'United Kingdom' and 'English'. Here you can learn from the provider how to use the site.

You can test your Amazon or eBay account by selling something from your home or garden. To get a quick sale, look up an item you want to sell on Amazon, and in the right hand column of the screen, click 'sell yours'. This gives you the sales ranking of that product so you will know whether it is a good seller or a poor seller. (The highest rank is number one). This will give you an idea of how easy it will be to sell your similar product on Amazon. Follow the instructions and you will be on your way.

The ease of use of these platforms means that you can make your fortune from anywhere in the world. The world has become a global village.

So what do you sell in order to make a fortune on Amazon or eBay? I do not suggest that you sell all the contents of your home or garden! In any event, selling your household contents will not make you a fortune. This is where 'drop shipping' comes in. Drop shipping is selling products that you do not need to stock and will be discussed later.

Alternatively, if you have some cash, you may decide to invest in www.alibaba.com to source products from around the world to sell. You do not even need to stock them at home, some of these companies provide drop shipping. There is also the option of fulfilment by Amazon. Learn all about this option from Amazon. Under the heading 'Make Money with Us', you will find 'Fulfilment by Amazon'. Click on that link to learn all about it.

CHAPTER 4

Domain Names

To have a website for your products you must have three things: a domain name, a website, and web hosting. A domain name is the name of your website, such as www.bestbuybooks.org. You need to find out if the name you intend to use is available, as someone else may already be using the name you are thinking about.

Most companies offering free websites or webhosting will allow you to choose your own domain name, assuming you've searched the Internet to ensure that the name is still available. Once you have confirmed that the name is available, purchase that name immediately because people and companies keep an eye out for the website names being searched for on the Internet and purchase that name before you can. Then they offer to sell it back to you at a higher price than you would have paid had you bought it right away.

Before you purchase a domain name for your website, explore how often the words you plan to use as part of your domain name are searched for on the Internet. You can do this by visiting http://adwords.google.co.uk/o/Targeting/Explorer?__c=100000 0000&__u=1000000000&ideaRequestType=KEYWORD_ID EAS.

Looking for search terms will help you determine whether the name you have chosen will prove effective. The more people search for a word on the Internet, the more likely it is that they will find your site if it has that word or phrase incorporated into its domain name.

The tool at www.googlekeywordtool.com provides a monthly and an annual breakdown of how many times people have searched for the words you are thinking of using as part of your domain name. It also reveals how often users have searched for that word in the United Kingdom (if that is the market you are interested in) and globally. This is useful information to assist you with choosing the most appropriate name for your website.

Click on the words 'Google Keyword Tool'. The words 'Find Keywords' appears. In the box below these words, type in the word or phrase you plan to use for your website. Follow the instructions on the rest of the page and click 'Search'. The result will tell you how often the words or phrase you plan to use for your website are searched for on the Internet. Check the monthly and global results. Some suggest that you should choose words that have a medium search result because worlds with a high search result probably have considerable competition from websites that use those words.

Use this tool in relation to each word or phrase you intend to use for your website. For example, if you plan to use the name www.bestbuybooks (and it is available as a domain name), type the words or phrase into the search box. If the search result shows that the words you have inputted are used frequently, you have made a great choice that will assist you with what is called search engine optimization, and the name of your website is likely to come up in a search, as people often use these words to search for the products pertaining to your website. Isn't that great? It is all *free*!

Remember that the website www.goolgekeywordtool.com also contains many free Google products that you can access *freely* and use to your advantage. This even includes free websites. What better place to display your products than on Google, the world's most popular search engine?

Now that you have determined what your domain name is, let's take a look at websites and webhosting.

CHAPTER 5

Free Websites

There are several providers of free websites. Once you have a website, you will need a host for it, which is likely to cost you a little money.

Some websites offer free websites and hosting, but be sure to read their terms and conditions carefully. You will need to ascertain whether the free website provided is suitable for promoting your business in the manner in which you intend to promote your products. For example, are you able to upload your product name and description? Does the site allow customers to buy your products from the site? Does the site allow you to link with PayPal to provide secure money transfers? The sites here are free websites, but it is up to you to ascertain whether they meet your requirements:

www.one.com

www.web.com

www.wix.com – This site has had five-star reviews.

www.moonfruit.com

www.magentocommerce.com

www.google.com/sites – Google has a video to explain the process to you.

Although some sites may allow you to build a free website and register your domain name, they will charge you for hosting, so be sure to take a careful look at their hosting packages.

CHAPTER 6

Web Hosting

Once you have your domain name and website, web hosting need not cost too much. Work with your budget, and search the Internet to find free web hosting options, such as www.wix.com, www.one.com, and www.web.com. When you have exhausted this search, you may wish to consider some other options that are compatible with your budget. However, guard against companies that contact you offering training and assistance, as they often charge a substantial amount after you have registered to use their service. Unless this approach is your preferred option and you can afford it, do not get bullied into it by promises of great financial reward. The only one benefiting financially is the company that is asking you for your credit card information and getting you into debt. Do not fall for it.

Some reasonable webhosting options are:

www.godaddy.com

www.google.com/sites

www.lunarpages.com

Scroll down the page to select basic web hosting or another option that suits your needs. The basic web hosting starts at $4.95 per month or approximately £3.12. If you are on a shoestring budget, this is sure to come in as a reasonable price.

Other options include www.hostgator.com, which offers web hosting starting from $3.96 (£2.50) per month. It is important to understand just what you're paying for; whichever web hosting company you join, it is important that its package is compatible with your needs.

Should you decide to sell a product or service as an affiliate marketer, you will need to be able to place links from that company and coupons from their site onto your website. Remember to join the affiliate programme of the company whose products you will be promoting, and wait for approval from that company in response to your application before placing links from that company onto your website.

Once you have decided on your website name and hosting package, remember to submit your website to the search engines. Search Google for 'how to submit your website to search engines'. Some companies charge you a small fee to do it for you, but you can submit your website to Yahoo, MSN, and Google free of charge. Submitting your website to as many search engines as possible will automatically increase your search engine ranking. Remember that the easier it is for customers to find you, the more business you are likely to get and the more successful you are likely to be.

CHAPTER 7

Affiliate Marketing and Affiliate Programmes

Affiliate marketing is selling companies' products on your website, and you are paid by commission by the company whose products you sell. For example, if you were to become an Amazon affiliate, you could sell Amazon products on your website and be paid a commission by Amazon for all sales that originate from your website.

In order to become an affiliate, you will need to visit the website www.amazon.com or www.amazon.co.uk. At the bottom of the page, you will see the heading, 'Make Money with Us'. In that list of options is 'Associates Programme'. Amazon will teach you how to use its links, banners, widgets, and aStore for *free*, and it will assist you in identifying weekly deals and staying connected with its discussion board and associates' blog.

With some forms of affiliate marketing, you are required to have a website to display your chosen products. On Amazon you have the option of creating an aStore and linking or embedding the link to your website. This is also a good way to get Amazon products on your website without maintaining any stock yourself.

Commission Junction

Another link for affiliate marketing is commission junction (www.cj.com). Once you're on the site, click on your region to get started. This is an excellent site to spend time studying. On this site, those who earn commissions are called 'publishers'. If this is what you want to do, click the yes option.

Take time to learn how to use the site properly before you get started. You must register with Commission Junction to obtain the login details that give you access to the advertisers. Please ensure that you apply to their programme and await the response before placing their links or coupons on your website.

It is best to have a website on which you can place external links and that links you to Twitter and Facebook. In this way you can share your products and your site with your friends and family and the world.

CHAPTER 8

Drop Shipping

When I first heard this term, I was curious to know what it was all about. Acting as a drop shipper is a way to earn money using the Internet without having to buy and hold stock. You advertise the goods on eBay or Amazon, or your own website, are paid by a purchaser, and forward the purchaser's details to the company that's holding the stock so they can ship it out to the customer. You then purchase the goods your customer ordered. With this process, you can set your own price within reason, pay the main company its price, and pocket the difference. All you need to do is learn how to list your products on Amazon, eBay, or your own website, and learn how to use the supplier's website. Some drop shippers will charge you for joining their programme, and others will allow you to join and show you how to list their products on eBay for free.

www.dropshiponline.co.uk is an excellent staring point. It is *free* to join, and they give you access to all the training you need. There is no need to pay a fortune to learn how to make a fortune as a drop shipper, when you can learn it on this website.

Once you have registered on this site, as a drop shipper they give you permission to use their product images to assist you with listing their products on Amazon, eBay or your website. Amazon also keeps an extensive record of products and images, once you have found a product you want to offer for sale on Amazon it is likely that you will find an image of exactly the same product on Amazon. Some websites have rules about using their product images, so be sure to check that there is no restriction on doing so.

If there is no restriction on using the product image, on Amazon, click on the photograph of the product and on the right of the screen look for the words "sell yours". Click on those words to see the sales ranking of that product and list it for sale.

Remember that you need an Amazon seller account to sell products on Amazon. This can be obtained by following the instructions on Amazon.

Most drop shippers will use discreet plain wrapping with your own details on the invoice. This will ensure your customers are not aware that you do not stock the goods. The important thing is that you meet their expectations and any delivery deadlines.

The advantages of drop shipping are that it enables you to start your own home-based business, at minimal cost, be your own boss and spend more time with your family. You do not need to sell a minimum or maximum but can work full time or part time depending on your needs.

Apart from being platforms on which you list your items for sale, Amazon and eBay, are also vital platforms from which to assess the competition. Should you see a product you are interested in selling on Amazon or eBay, you can use the site to see how well that product is selling. This will enable you to assess whether you can compete profitably. When setting your price, do not forget to factor in the cost of shipping the product and fees payable to Amazon or eBay upon sale.

All that is left to do now is find the products that give you a competitive edge and list them. There are many drop shippers out there, they are easy to find on Google or any of the other search engines. You do not need to limit your search to drop shippers in the UK. Your aim is profit, so your only concern should be whether you are able to meet the delivery targets to enable you to provide a first-class service to your customers.

Links to wholesalers and drop shippers can be found on Google or any search engine. Some examples are the following:

- www.dhgate.com – This site promises drop shipping direct from China.
- www.wholesaleforum.com/Dropshippers – This website confirms that new online retailers can turn over 3 million dollars in sales by applying drop shipping correctly and using reliable suppliers.
- www.wholesaledeals.co.uk
- www.dinobulk.com

Please remember that the author of this e-book is not associated with or an agent of any of the websites featured in the book. Please exercise your own due diligence when joining or registering with any site.

Most of this information is freely available, but you may need to pay a small fee to register with the website.

CHAPTER 9

Doing Business as a Company

Whether you do business as a sole trader or as an affiliate, you may wish to consider doing business as a company. Trading as a company adds a bit of clout and gives your trading partners a way to check on you at Companies House. In short, it adds credibility. Especially when it comes to drop shipping, you may wish to consider the option of doing business as a company because drop shippers are also wholesalers and prefer to do business with other companies, rather than individuals.

Visit www.companiedhouse.co.uk to set up a limited company in the United Kingdom. On the toolbar, click 'Start a Company'. This will take you to a page showing you all you need to have in place and do to start a company.

Trading under a company name has benefits, such as lower taxation, but it also has its responsibilities. You can learn all about your responsibilities as a director from Companies House, which will also keep you up to date on your responsibilities. Explore this site and you will find all you need to know to set up a limited liability company here in the UK for less than £20.00.

Another useful source of information can be found at www.startupbritain.org. You will need to register with this site to gain access to all the information. There are many advertisers on the site, and I caution you about using this site, as many of the advertisers are not free and may offer services that require more than a limited budget. Please take your time to examine what is available.

However, the site provides a wealth of information about websites, advertising, and other subjects of interest to any budding entrepreneur.

Once you have formed your company, you should also be able to secure a business bank account. This is where www.startupbritain.co.uk proves very helpful, as it provides information about banking. You can always visit your local bank to makes enquires, but you can also link directly to a bank of your choice and get the information you need online.

If you are living or working in another country, similar services will be available to you there. Check out your local Companies House, and your local bank to find out what services they offer.

Do take time to read through all the options to ensure that you are not being charged for having the account before you start making any money. Some banks charge businesses for simply having a business bank account. Penalties and fines are also more severe for businesses, so please take a moment to understand what is being offered and to read the fine print.

Once your business and bank account has been set up, you are ready to trade.

CHAPTER 10

Sourcing Products to Retail

If drop shipping is not for you, you may wish to source products locally or abroad for retail. The websites for this is www.alibaba.com and www.aliexpress.com

If you already know your niche—(that is, what you want to sell, to whom you want to sell it, and where to find them), then alibaba.com can help you find the cheapest suppliers.

This book is mainly about just how much you can learn from the Internet for free. If you are sourcing products for retail, you will certainly need to pay suppliers to send you their goods. However, alibaba.com has an escrow account service that will help you limit your risk in the unlikely event that you deal with someone without integrity. The escrow service will hold the funds you pay until you confirm you have received the goods you purchased. The site also ranks its suppliers, so you will know whether you are dealing with a company whose credibility and reliability have been verified.

You can sell these products on your own website, on Amazon, or on eBay.

EBay is another source of suppliers. All you need to do to source products from eBay—(products that may already be right here in the UK)—is to visit www.ebay.com. Under the 'categories', scroll down to 'wholesale and job lots'. You never know: you may find what you are looking for there.

If you decide to go down the route of international sourcing of products, you may need an import license or to pay import duties once the goods are received into the United Kingdom, or your country. You can visit Her Majesty's Revenue and Customs at: https://www.gov.uk/government/organisations/hm-revenue-customs to assist you in this process if you are living in the UK. (If you live elsewhere, your local customs and excise may be able to assist you). In the search panel, look up 'customs handling of import and export freight'. There you will find a wealth of information about importing products into the United Kingdom and restrictions. The rules for products that originate in the European Community differ from those for products that originate from elsewhere.

You can also learn how to obtain an 'economic operation registration and identification number', or EORI. This number means that you will be recognized as an Authorized Economic Operator or AEO. You will also find relevant forms, which can be submitted electronically. There is just so much information on this site and it is all *free*. If you are patient and eager to understand your responsibilities and expand your expertise, you will find all you need to know here.

Chapter 8 pointed you to other sources from which you may find a host of wholesalers and discusses drop shippers and wholesalers in detail. You may also wish to visit international trade fairs where suppliers display their products to find a product of interest to you.

If you have written a book and are interested in marketing it yourself, you may need to get it into print. Alibaba.com can help you find printers anywhere in the world. These printers can give you a quote for printing your book and shipping it to you. All you need to verify is the customs duty on books once they have arrived in your county and the transportation cost of getting the books or shipment to you. This is a sure way to save on the printing cost of your book. Why not give it a try? You can always order a print sample before you make the final decision to have your work printed abroad.

CHAPTER 11

Getting into Stores

You may wonder what to do if you already have your own product. Perhaps you are passionate about your product but have not been able to get it into the retail stores.

The competition for retail space is fierce, so you must be proactive and professional if you really want to get your product in the door and on the shelf.

Here is a checklist to success in selling your own product. Put the checklist into a notebook so you can tick what you have completed and take notes to refresh your mind later. Our lives are dynamic and we get distracted easily, but making notes lets us pick up from where we left off.

1. Does your product have a UPC or barcode? If not, get one. Simply Google 'how to obtain a barcode or UPC'. Retailers will need this to stock your product.

2. Research the retailers to whom you would like to sell your product. When researching a retailer, think about who their buyers are and how to reach them. If you are not able to find this information on their website, you may send an email to ask how to contact them to pitch your product.

3. Why do you want to sell your product to those specific retailers? Knowing the answer to this question will give you a ready answer when you write or approach the retailer about why you would like to display and sell your product in their store. In the process of formulating this answer, you will have thought about their customers and how your product meets their needs.

4. Research your competition. It helps to know what your competitors are offering and how your product differs from theirs. In particular, what advantages does it have over your competitor's products? How can weaknesses in your product be overcome? Why, despite knowing these weaknesses exist, have you not sought to improve

your product? When researching your competitors, take note of their packaging and how you may improve your packaging. Retailers are looking for goods that appeal to the eye so they 'fly off the shelf', so take time to provide the right packaging. Why do you want to sell your product to those specific retailers? Knowing the answer to this question will give you a ready answer when you write or approach the retailer about why you would like to display and sell your product in their store. In the process of formulating this answer, you will have thought about their customers and how your product meets their needs.

5. Develop a product sheet/line sheet that tells the buyer what you are offering. This sheet is, essentially, a flyer that advertises your product. It should have your company name and your logo at the top. The body should contain pictures of your product, the various colours and sizes offered, the name of the piece, a short description, the wholesale price, and the recommended retail price. Below your photographs set out the terms, conditions, and payment methods, penalties for late

payment, and any return policy. At the bottom place a footer with your contact details, website address, and email address.

6. Ensure that you have an order form. You will need one of these online if you if you have a website, but if you are relying on fax, you will need a hard copy.

7. Write your sales pitch. Your sales pitch should be personal to the retailer you are targeting, rather than a general pitch that applies to everyone. Retailers will know whether what they have received is a template you use for all retailers or whether you have taken some time, based on your research, to address their store in particular. At the very least, get the name of the purchasing manager for each retailer.

8. Your sales pitch can read something like this:

Dear Mr/Ms _____

I am writing to you on behalf of _____ (Company Name), for which I am the managing director. My company would like to introduce you to a few of our products.

I recently visited your website and online store and thought that our line of products would make a perfect addition to your current line. Currently I am promoting_____, which is _____. I believe that your customers will appreciate the _____of our product range, hence this letter. (Elaborate on the features of your product.)

I would be happy to send you a free sample/please find enclosed a free sample of our product, which demonstrates the features. My product has had several reviews in the local and international press, and I enclose here a few copies of these reviews.

I have a line sheet/product and order form ready for your review. Simply reply to (provide your email address or phone), and I will be happy to email or fax them to you.

Thank you for taking the time to consider our offerings. I look forward to hearing from you.
Sincerely,

Your name
Your Company Name

9. Track your enquiries. It is annoying for your potential customer to phone and you don't know which products you have asked them to consider. Create a table or planner that looks something like this:

Date	Company Name	Contact Name	Letter sent	Follow up date	Orders received	Delivery date

Following these suggestions will help ensure that your product gets the attention it deserves.

CHAPTER 12

Marketing

As the aim of this book is to show you just how much you can learn for *free* over the Internet, I encourage you to market your book or products on the Internet—for *free*.

Set up a Facebook page, Twitter and Pinterest account for your book or product. Sites like Amazon also have author pages that can be used effectively to promote your book, should you have one.

Should you have any difficulty performing any of these tasks, visit www.youtube.com and search using the words 'how to'. For example, if you want to set up a Pinterest account but do not understand how to do so, type in 'how to set up a Pinterest account'. You are sure to find someone who explains the process on video and shows you how it is done. Do the same should you want to learn how to create a Facebook page or a Twitter account. You can also learn how to sell e-books on eBay. One can learn just about anything here.

Do not forget to investigate all of Google's free products, as well as their pay-per-click program, called Google Adwords. This may boost your business, but you do have to pay for it.

One way to assist with your marketing is to give away free e-books about topics related to your product or service. This is a marketing tool used by many companies, including small businesses and artists. Many companies also give away free e-books when you subscribe to their websites. Many e-books that you may want to use have already been created, and you can find them at http://getaproduct.info/wp-login.php?redirect_to=%2. After registering, you will have access to articles about how successfully e-books are being used in marketing. You can even sell these e-books should you wish to do so. They cover a wide range of topics. All you need to do is choose the one that is appropriate to the product or service which you are offering and offer it to your customers free in exchange for their subscribing to your newsletter or to say thank you for visiting your site.

This is not the only site that offers free e-books. You can find more options by searching on Google.

We all love freebies. Why not use them to boost your marketing campaign?

:

CHAPTER 13

Some Helpful Tips

Here are some tips to help you along your way.

Tip 1

Keep your home address private.

As this is a work-from-home book, you may wish to keep your home address private by obtaining a post-box address for your business, by visiting www.poboxes.com. if you live and operate in the UK. If you are operating from elsewhere, your local post office will be able to assist you or there may be websites in your country offering post box services.

You can also Google 'how to obtain a post box address', which will give you several choices. There is also the 'old faithful' Royal Mail at www.royalmail.com. Remember that there is a charge for post-boxes; none are free.

Tip 2

Pay your taxes.

As you are now running your own business you will need to pay taxes on whatever profit you make. Should you wish to take charge of paying taxes yourself, you can get help from Her Majesty's Revenue and Customs or buy some simple bookkeeping books from your local book shop or online from www.taxcafe.com.

One sure way of keeping your records straight for the tax- man is to keep records of all your income for each month in one place, such as in a folder or envelope, and all your expenses in another. This means that you will soon have twenty-four folders/envelopes, twelve of which represents your income for each month and twelve of which containing your expense receipts for each month. Clearly, you need pay no one for this approach!

You can also buy an accounting software package or hire a bookkeeper or an accountant. You can always be your own accountant, keeping track of your expenses and income. A simple Google search of the words 'basic accounting packages' can find you hundreds. You are guaranteed to find one in this list to suit your needs and your budget.

Tip 3

Be smart about postage.

If you are selling on Amazon or eBay and you are doing the posting yourself, it all works out nicely if all you need to post is no larger than an A4-sized envelope. However, should you need to post bulkier items and arrange swift delivery to meet deadlines, you will need the help of a professional and reliable postage and delivery service.

It is useful to arrange postage with one or more carriers, such as Parcel Force, UPS, or DHL, if you intend to post bulky items and are working from home. These companies usually need a telephone number to be able to contact the customer and ensure delivery, so be sure that you obtain this information from your customers when they purchase an item. The carriers also require the weight, height, and depth of an item, which you can find on Amazon for identical products.

Tip 4

Identify your own products for international sales.

If you are an international seller selling your own products on Amazon, be sure to obtain an International standard book number or ISBN for books and barcode for other products.

Tip 5

Space your work and achievements.

Do not try to achieve all of this in one sitting. Your goal is to reach the end but you need to go through the process. The process can be long and tedious depending on your level of expertise, knowledge and ability to use Internet. So give yourself time to reach and achieve each milestone.

Tip 6

Your mindset matter.

Remember that the world has become a global village. You can achieve anything your want once you set your mind to it. You will not achieve what you want out of life by sitting on your couch at home or by complaining about the world around you. Every success requires you to make the effort and put some work into it. There is no need for you to be broke, frustrated and angry. This book covers the basic ground - work for you, you only need to build from here. Maintain a positive mindset and work at your goal in small chunks one day at a time.

CHAPTER 14

What Next?

What happens next depends on you. I hope that, having read this book, you will be able to formulate your ideas or that you have already decided what your business will entail. I also hope that you have decided to get started right away.

Get a notebook and write down what you think you would like to do and how you would like to achieve it. Remember to think big, but start small, especially if you do not have a lot of capital to get started. On one side of your notebook, make a list of things to do. Then turn the book over, treating the back as if it were the front, and make a note of all the websites you intend to visit or have visited and registered with, as it is ever so easy to lose track of all the user names and passwords you have used. You will also need to keep track of all the sites you have found particularly useful. You may do so by bookmarking them, but it is also useful to keep a note of what was helpful on that site and why.

Now find yourself a comfortable chair, place your laptop in a comfortable position, and get cracking. Use Google, Yahoo, or MSN to start searching the net for whatever you are interested in and can learn for free.

If you have decided to write a book, commit to a few quiet hours a day and see the book through to the end.

Commit to finishing each stage of your task before moving on. This will give you time to see how you are developing and improving from day to day and drawing nearer to your goal of making a living from the comfort of your own home or anywhere in the world.

Good Luck!

I hope you have enjoyed reading this book and have found it useful in helping you live your dream. If you have found this book useful, visit my facebook page, give me a like and share my link with your friends and invite your friends to like my book page https://www.facebook.com/pages/Deborah-Bowers/305156936286593?ref=hl and follow me on Twitter @bowers_deborah.

Other books by Deborah Bowers:

The Circle of Love